Survive the Season

Cover and Interior designed by De'Juan McDuell

First Edition, 2021.

Umoja Publishing
Umoja.Publishing@gmail.com
Valparaiso, IN 46383

Survive the Season

De'Juan V. McDuell

Umoja
Publishing

Dedication

This book is dedicated to my mom, Glenda, who always told me I could be anything and my wife, Jen, who helped me prove to myself that it was true.

May God bless the souls of those taken away from us by irresponsible hands.

Black Lives Matter

Table of Contents

Detroit, Yesterday

Where I'm from, hollow speeches are spoken
in tattered forms of American English
and broken up by thunderous claps
that have nothing to do with storm clouds
or audience applause.

Here, the echoes in the distance, panged
voices of our history, strike
like union workers fighting
for fair wages, better health,
care, and working conditions.

Here, opportunity rarely knocks
on the fabricated refuge of wrought iron bars;
off-putting, discouraging intimate interactions
with interlopers and benefactors, alike
in their untrustworthy being.

Hear sirens scream into the night with urgency,
arriving onsite too late to see the moment -
our loved ones have passed. Early editions
report bad news that lasts five days; a torsion of torment
and anguish. There were less and less to places to live despite
flight. There were less and less places for work, but night
concealed the pain of our sins, huddled us close, gave us fire,
warmed us, showed us how to love, and taught us how to
pray for tomorrow.

Sanctuary

I bumped my head a million times on that table,
Grandma's dining room table

For everyone else it was a place to eat,
But for me it was a place of peace.

I watched a world that had nothing to do with me, yet I could
not avert my eyes.
I listened to the murmur of voices that seemed so far away.
I smelled the sweet aroma of love rise from plates of yams,
fried fish, and collard greens.

And I thought.

I spent somber instances silently, mulling over cold mornings,
reading, rainbow money, cartoons, and the music that filled
my mind.
I was never too young or too poor; it was perfect there.

I sat there after Granddad won the lottery:
All that money spread across the table-
Looking from below was like
Being lost in a familiar forest.

I was sitting there countless times
When my mom yelled, "Get Down!"
Bullets never broke my barrier.
But I was hit hard when

Reality riddled my young mind with worry.
Amidst the mess of what remained,
My mother cataloged what was missing.

That brown box of hope with a bent wire antenna and one knob gone
All that I knew of fine food was pilfered from our freezer.
Everything worth anything.
And the only thing I remember calling my own.

My brush: Plastic and purple with scratches, worn bristles, fuzz.

I was there when I realized
I wasn't safe there.

DWB

I don't drive fancy, but I drive fast,
and every time I pass a cop my life flashes
back to the first time I was ever pulled over
for being Black.

I remember the alternating red & blue
and the blinding brightness of the white
aimed at illuminating the uncertainty of our blackness;
Sharpie black - Come see the permanence
of the marks we make on the world.

Afraid of the dark,
the slave patrol always carries extra light,
burning effigies of us in their minds, probably
imagining the woodie wagon as kindling.

He asks Grandma for her license and registration,
Walks away to run plates, spins lies
upon his return about this car matching the description
of a stolen vehicle.

60-something knowing eyes,
saddened by this reality,
become precursors to the verbal warning -
"Turn that cap 'round."

Drawing Home

Cement floors carpeted by crushed ice that won't melt
Reality hung on walls like murals, as if rendered by
Rembrandt
A sky-blue ceiling rubbed gray by a dirty eraser

This is home.

From a distance, he could trace
the outlines of dilapidated structures –
Burn victims on their last legs, threatening to fall.

Supported by two hundred six
beams, their skin pronounces their shapes
as they breathe deep sighs of captivity. Blood
stained glass splashes color on the otherwise
dismal scene.

He – unaware of his own art,
Clutches the bucket
As the light adjusts
Its contrast –
Green > Yellow > Red
"Roses for sale."

After the Storm

Tell them this is all a dream.
Visions of death still float
into their minds, numbing
their ability to wade
through this life. They inhale a thick

air that saturates
their lungs - trying to hold
their heads high enough for someone
to see that they are engulfed
by inadequacy.

Home is where hearts sank
under twenty feet of water, washed away
with memories and medication. Some died,
but are not considered a victims of Katrina
or this government's ineptitude.

They "live" in houses that lack
power and water or in trailers that measure
240 square feet – Scarcely enough room for one person,
many share this deficient
space with five or six other broken hearts.
Tell them this is a dream.

They will close their heavy
eyes, wishing the weight of reality away
from their shoulders. Sinking into broken slumber,
few will awake with new spirit

as if baptized by flood waters because
this is not a dream.

They Wanted Change

I stopped to drop a couple quarters in his cup, averting
my eyes from his unfocused gaze. I was amazed
by the way his back curved under the weight
of summer heat as beads of sweat crept down his forehead.
His life was gray.

Cluttered streets clattered with chatter as his Styrofoam rattled
metallic smatterings of hope. The irrational sound followed
hollow steps across the bridge joining voices promoting
foods, water, soaps, and incense provoking No's from my shaking
head. They were selling themselves.

I bought drinks and snacks from the racks of a local store
as a memory brought the rattle back. The jangle rang with the abundance
of poverty and made my water taste bitter. Slakeless, I walked back
through the network of street merchants searching the skies for reasons
to avoid judging eyes. All they wanted was change.

Salutations

Yesterday, you asked how I felt, and I wanted to tell you the truth –

That muffled sounds created by closed hands
thump like the soundtrack to my life and repeat erratically.

That my ears ring with nightmarish howls of anger
dangling like lifeless bodies that sway
from sturdy beams in broken homes.

I wanted to show you the bruises on my body –
deep purples that match wilted African violets,
fading into faint smears of dandelion residue.

I wanted to tell you how I planned to leave him –
to gather my courage and my clothes, but instead my abandoned ambitions
Hang like shame and point like the clock hands that glide across faces
when I search for time to help with homework,
shop for groceries, pay bills, and find a place to feel safe.

I wanted to say forsaken, forlorn, frail, fatigued, defeated, but instead
I said, "Fine."

Persona Non Grata

They labeled me a wanna-be
when I just wanted to Be
Common, Kweli, Nas, or Yaasin. I wanted to be happy in my
skin, I wanted to be thin, I wanted a crew of friends to say we
were "thick as thieves"
In the night, I wanted to dream of light and breathe to write
and grieve
The lives and loss of my homies to enemies
in different colors and cross my heart, swearing that I would
retaliate.

I wanted to talk black and to be
phat as Adidas laces and trace my trauma
beyond living in the burbs with a single mama.
They call it survivor's guilt and I just wanted
to know that my tears are worth the same
as those flowers that were
left in the hood to wilt.

The House of Torturous Love

That bed of roses was coercion covered in petals that failed to
soften the jabs of sharp barbs. Careless remarks abrade the
fabric of self-worth and grate
at nerves creating tears
and alcohol sweats.

Listen.

Lessons lie in listlessness, where drunken statements stagger
up splintering staircases;
where sober judgments creep into mind
and compromise the structure
Of an already-weakened psyche
holding contempt. Every day, scorn burns
without remedy; floors groan
from years of thankless servitude; doors swing with whining
sighs, dodging jagged ridicule
being hurled from room to room.

Couch cushions slump low from depression, permanently
scarred by embers and hot ash, rendered so by negligent
hands, deliberate fingertips.

Nails would snag if walls could talk
you into leaving. They can't.
So, you stay.

Escape Capsule (a sestina)

Somewhere amid towering construction
and unyielding gray carpeting lies
a small, pliable body. Her beautiful face
displays a countenance of blue,
swaying on uncertainty, trying not to fall.
She reflects on pools of self-contempt with newly dried eyes.

Unable to hide the fear in her eyes,
she wearily views the world and its construction.
Her once stable world begins to fall.
Feeling betrayed, she lies
to herself to cope with abuse from Dad. Blue
pills are her only haven as strives to save face.

The clock reads six thirty. It is time for her to face
fears. Trying to escape blurred lines, her eyes
frisk the tablets impatiently. Soothing blue
capsules take her to safety drawn on construction
paper when she was young. Before there were lies,
there was love to catch her should she fall.

So many things had changed since Fall.
Feeling anxious before graduation, trying to face
a world that makes her sick, she lies
comfortably sinking into plush carpet. Her eyes
take in the fabric's construction.
Each twist of the strands reminds her of blue

whirlpools and dueling currents. She was not blue
back when seas were calm. She was happy to fall
from her chariot into aquatic wonder. Construction
of water molecules were no concern during face-
offs against this stranger who had her eyes.
No more tears. No movements. No more lies

can be told to her, for she lies
guarded from victimizers. Her body rested on blue
carpet, as light abandoned her eyes.
She did not falter in the slowness of her fall.
Color crept from her face,
seeming to alter its construction.

Here lies the lost beneath the leaves that fall.
Once blue, she shines with peace upon her face
Her eyes, like stars, remain a light to new construction.

At a Loss

I've spent so many years bending
and stretching the English language
to fit the form of my emotions. Still,

I find myself a loss as I reach
through the recesses of my mind
only to reveal a singular,
"I'm sorry."

An inadequacy matched
only by hand towels
attempting to slow the currents
of a raging river.
You and I stand quietly
and remember –

We trade stories as alternate
food for thought, and go back
like easy chairs, but it's hard
to just sit, so we pace –

moving backward
through the corridors
of our minds trying to access
only the positive doorways
as the outlets that lead to this very moment.

This is the instance that I want
you to use my shoulders. I want
you to know that my hand is waiting for yours.

I want to illustrate my support,
so I ask that you draw
strength from my love.
Lean against me because, collectively,
We are strong.

Sundown

Gauzy pinks, vibrant oranges, and pastel purples draped the
dusk sky.

With extended wavelengths of light, the sun's rays probably
left him
longing for more peaceful moments to wander the memory
lane
that brought him to this point. He probably wondered,
his mind swirling with negativity, "Is this real?".

I can only hope serenity and prayers were disruptive to voices
tagging him with undue insults, injuries diminished by
epinephrine.
I hope his mind, heart, and spirit built tranquility into that
moment,
that he was able to rest quickly and rise like the sun shouting
Eloah.

Birds and Butterflies Endure

We, caged birds, sing for you today and, tomorrow,
mourning will come with dismay and tears, but still, we rise,
tearing ourselves from the bitter, selfish wishes
for you to come back. I, Miss Maya,
see nothing will work to cure
ache, but understanding the foundation
of transition is Love.

I can hear the song you sang, before you were a butterfly.

It told a story of selflessness, wisdom, strength. Phenomenal
woman slinging my favorite rhymes to heal wounded hearts
and bruised egos -
Educating us in the ways of nobility, showing the importance
of spirit, telling us,
Be Amazing!
Rise, Work, Dance, Love, Endure.

Allegory

I wish that I could write
a happy ending to this life.
Mending broken, blotted hearts
delivering some light-

to the depths of shaded souls
and shattered lives of battered wives-
to the drug addicted thugs convicted
lost in scattered lies-
to the haggard homeless masses
harassed for sleeping in the park-
to the little kids neglected
and ones molested in the dark-
to the junkies snorting caine
or pushing smack into their veins-
to hapless hookers smoking crack
to alleviate the pain.

This is for-

the lost and forgotten,
the dirty, sick, and rotten,
the "too poor to be" Americans
sleeping under boxes,
the mentally afflicted,
the righteous turned wicked,
the swept under the rug, never had a hug misfits,
the dispossessed, derelict, despondent, and dejected

the silver spoon-frying, crying, dying, and infected.

And this is for my audience
who might be none of the above
living little happy endings
because of someone's love.

About the Author

De'Juan McDuell is a poet, writer, and the author of the poetry collection, *Survive the Season*. De'Juan is a lifelong writer and has continually sharpened his focus on the details of his subjects in his poetry. When he's not busy bending meaning, twisting words, and turning phrases, De'Juan enjoys going on adventures with his wife and daughter.

Made in the USA
Middletown, DE
19 February 2022

61410310R00017